BALLPARK GREATS

PRO BASEBALL'S BEST PLAYERS

JUSTIN VERLANDER

GREG BACH

BALLPARK GREATS

PRO BASEBALL'S BEST PLAYERS

CHRISTIAN YELICH

JUSTIN VERLANDER

MAX SCHERZER

MIKE TROUT

NOLAN ARENADO

BALLPARK GREATS

PRO BASEBALL'S BEST PLAYERS

JUSTIN VERLANDER

GREG BACH

MASON CREST
PHILADELPHIA
MIAMI

Mason Crest
450 Parkway Drive, Suite D
Broomall, Pennsylvania 19008
(866) MCP-BOOK (toll-free)
www.masoncrest.com

First printing
9 8 7 6 5 4 3 2 1

ISBN (hardback) 978-1-4222-4438-8
ISBN (series) 978-1-4222-4434-0
ISBN (ebook) 978-1-4222-7373-9

Library of Congress Cataloging-in-Publication Data

Names: Bach, Greg, author.
Title: Justin Verlander / Greg Bach.
Description: Broomall, Pennsylvania : Mason Crest, 2020. | Series: Ballpark greats : pro baseball's best players | Includes bibliographical references and index.
Identifiers: LCCN 2019046507 | ISBN 9781422244388 (hardback) | ISBN 9781422273739 (ebook)
Subjects: LCSH: Verlander, Justin—Juvenile literature. | Pitchers (Baseball)—United States—Biography—Juvenile literature. | Baseball players—United States—Biography—Juvenile literature.
Classification: LCC GV865.V44 B34 2020 | DDC 796.357092 [B]—dc23
LC record available at https://lccn.loc.gov/2019046507

Developed and Produced by National Highlights Inc.
Editor: Andrew Luke
Production: Crafted Content LLC

QR CODES AND LINKS TO THIRD-PARTY CONTENT

CONTENTS

KEY ICONS TO LOOK FOR:

 Words to Understand: These words with their easy-to-understand definitions will increase the reader's understanding of the text, while building vocabulary skills.

 Sidebars: This boxed material within the main text allows readers to build knowledge, gain insights, explore possibilities, and broaden their perspectives by weaving together additional information to provide realistic and holistic perspectives.

 Educational Videos: Readers can view videos by scanning our QR codes, providing them with additional educational content to supplement the text. Examples include news coverage, moments in history, speeches, iconic sports moments, and much more!

 Text-Dependent Questions: These questions send the reader back to the text for more careful attention to the evidence presented there.

 Research Projects: Readers are pointed toward areas of further inquiry connected to each chapter. Suggestions are provided for projects that encourage deeper research and analysis.

 Series Glossary of Key Terms: This back-of-the-book glossary contains terminology used throughout this series. Words found here increase the reader's ability to read and comprehend higher-level books and articles in this field.

WORDS TO UNDERSTAND

flirt with: to come close to reaching or experiencing something

resounding: unequivocal; emphatic

unfathomable: not possible to understand; incomprehensible

CHAPTER 1

GREATEST MOMENTS

MASTERFUL IN THE MOTOR CITY

Justin Verlander's arrival for spring training with the Detroit Tigers in 2006 was accompanied with questions galore. His only previous major league appearances were his first two big league starts during the 2005 season, in which he coughed up a combined nine runs and 15 hits in less than 12 innings of work while throwing a wild pitch and hitting a batter, too. The second overall pick in the 2004 draft had lots to prove when he stepped into the Lakeland, Florida, sunshine. And boy, did Verlander ever deliver in **resounding** fashion.

Verlander seized a spot in Detroit's starting rotation when the 2006 regular season began. He went out and won his first start in Texas with a dominating seven shutout innings, allowing just two hits while whiffing seven. The 89 pitches he threw that evening provided a glimpse of his greatness and were the starting point of his hike through baseball's record books. Verlander won 17 games that season, tied for most on the Tigers' staff, and captured the American League's (AL) Rookie of the Year award. Those 17 wins were also the most by an AL Rookie of the Year pitcher since Mark "The Bird" Fidrych won 19 games back in 1976, also with the Tigers.

During nearly 13 seasons in the Motor City, Verlander led Major League Baseball (MLB) in strikeouts and innings pitched three times and in wins twice. In 2011, he put up monster numbers rarely seen, going 24–5 with 250 strikeouts and a 2.40 earned run average to win the Cy Young Award. In fact, he was so good that he won the American League's Most Valuable Player (MVP) award too, becoming only the 10th pitcher in MLB history to pull off that double.

AMAZING ASTRO

After being dealt to Houston late in the 2017 season as part of the Tigers' rebuilding efforts, all Verlander did upon his arrival was go 5–0 in the regular

GREATEST CAREER MOMENTS

HERE IS A LIST OF SOME OF VERLANDER'S CAREER FIRSTS AND GREATEST ACHIEVEMENTS DURING HIS TIME IN MLB:

THROWS FIRST NO-HITTER

A twenty-four-year-old Verlander, in the middle of just his second season in the major leagues, tossed a no-hitter against the National League Central Division–leading Milwaukee Brewers on June 12, 2007, in Detroit's 4–0 win. Marking just the second complete game of his young career, he had 12 strikeouts and issued four walks in becoming the first Detroit pitcher since Jack Morris in 1984 to throw a no-hitter. Verlander's fastball was humming all night during his 112-pitch assault. He showed no signs of tiring as he hit 101 miles per hour on the radar gun in the ninth inning and struck out the first two hitters before getting J. J. Hardy to fly out to the right fielder Magglio Ordonez, sending Tigers' fans into celebration mode. Verlander's gem was the first no-hitter ever thrown at Comerica Park and the first by a Detroit pitcher at home since Virgil Trucks did it in 1952 at Briggs Stadium, the Tigers' home at that time.

When he blanked the Milwaukee Brewers in 2007, Justin Verlander became the first Detroit Tigers' pitcher to hurl a no-hitter since Jack Morris in 1984.

THROWS SECOND NO-HITTER

Nearly four years after throwing his first no-hitter, Verlander flirted with perfection on his way to notching a precious second no-hitter in a 9–0 win against Toronto on a Saturday afternoon during the 2011 season. In front of 23,453 at Rogers Centre in Toronto, he used a mid-90s fastball, mixed in with a slider and change-up, to keep Blue Jays' hitters off balance and off the bases. The only Toronto player to reach base was J. P. Arencibia, who was walked with one out in the eighth inning, erasing Verlander's bid for a perfect game. Verlander had to throw just 10 pitches in a pressure-filled ninth inning to secure the no-hitter. He got the first two batters out on a pop-up and ground out, and then struck out Rajai Davis (who would become his teammate in Detroit three years later) swinging to complete the historic afternoon. In major league history only 35 pitchers have thrown two or more no-hitters.

Justin Verlander collected the second no-hitter of his career against the Toronto Blue Jays during the 2011 season.

THROWS THIRD NO-HITTER

How's this for a 1–2–3 punch? Verlander threw his *first* no-hitter for the Astros, his *second* against Toronto, and the *third* no-hitter of his spectacular career, all in the span of two hours and 29 minutes. On the first day of September during the 2019 season. Verlander delivered a performance dipped in brilliance, striking out 14 batters and walking just one on his way to his third no-hitter and becoming just the sixth pitcher in major league history to throw three of them. He also became the third pitcher to no-hit the same team twice and the first to no-hit the same club twice on the road. With two outs in the top of the ninth inning of a scoreless game, Abraham Toro, appearing in just his eighth major league game, cracked a two-run home run to give Verlander and the Astros the margin they were looking for. Verlander sealed number three by getting Bo Bichette to ground out to third base.

Justin Verlander threw his third career no-hitter, and first as an Astro, in a 2–0 win against Toronto during the 2019 season.

WINS BOTH THE 2011 CY YOUNG *AND* MVP AWARDS

Justin Verlander was a one-man wrecking crew during the 2011 America League season, crushing batting averages and leaving a long list of frustrate and unsuccessful hitters in his wake. He won 24 games, was beaten just five times, and piled up 250 strikeouts on his way to being a unanimous Cy Youn Award selection. Those 24 wins were the most in the American League since Bob Welch went 27–6 for Oakland back in 1990. Verlander became the third Detroit pitcher to win the award, joining Denny McLain (1968 and 1969) and Guillermo Hernandez (1984). He also grabbed the American League MVP award, a rare double done only 10 times in MLB history. He joined this elite company in winning both honors: Don Newcombe (1956), Sandy Koufax (1963), Bob Gibson (1968), Denny McLain (1968), Vida Blue (1971), Rollie Fingers (1981), Willie Hernandez (1984), Roger Clemens (1986), and Dennis Eckersley (1992).

Justin Verlander won the Cy Young and MVP awards in 2011, only the 10th time that has been done in major league history.

WINS SECOND CY YOUNG AWARD

In 2019, Verlander was once again voted the winner of the AL Cy Young Award as the best pitcher in the league. He led the Major Leagues in wins, going 21–6 on the season. Verlander's 34 starts and 223 inning pitched were also the most in all of MLB, and he led all pitchers with a .803 WHIP as well. Toss in a career-high 300 strikeouts en route to an Astros playoff appearance, and his Cy Young worthiness could not be denied. It was, however, a very close decision, as Verlander beat teammate Gerrit Cole by just 12 points in the vote. At thirty-six years old, Verlander was the 20th pitcher to win multiple Cy Youngs, and the only one to have as many as eight seasons in between awards. At the beginning of the 2020 season, Verlander was the active leader in career wins and strikeouts.

MLB interviews Justin Verlander moments after he wins the 2019 AL Cy Young Award.

PICKS UP CAREER STRIKEOUT NUMBER 3,000

Verlander pitched a game typical of his 2019 season in a 6–3 Astros win against the Los Angeles Angels on September 28th. He threw six innings of four-hit ball, logging a dozen strikeouts for his MLB-leading 21st win of the season. Verlander entered the game with 2,994 career strikeouts, including 288 on the season. With this effort, he hit two significant milestones. Verlander surpassed the 300 strikeout mark in a season for the first time. Even more impressively, he became only the 18th pitcher all-time with more than 3,000 career strikeouts. The first 2,373 strikeouts of Verlander's career were delivered in a Detroit uniform. He became the active leader in career strikeouts following the 2019 season with the retirement of New York Yankees' lefthander CC Sabathia.

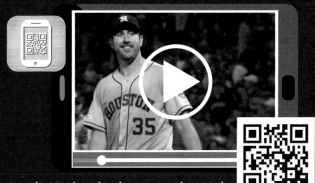

Justin Verlander became the 18th pitcher in major league history to join the 3,000-strikeout club when he fanned the Angels' Kole Calhoun during the 2019 season.

NAMED 2017 ALCS MVP

The Houston Astros acquired Justin Verlander for exactly these types of moments: big games with high stakes where every pitch is steeped in pressure and where one mistake can be a season-ender. He delivered and was sensational in the 2017 American League Championship Series (ALCS) against the New York Yankees, winning the ALCS MVP by going 2–0 with a 0.56 ERA. Verlander tossed a complete game gem in a 2–1 game 2 victory where 93 of the 124 pitches he threw were strikes. He relinquished only five hits while striking out 13. Five of those strikeouts came against the first two hitters in the New York lineup: Brett Gardner and Aaron Judge. He followed up that performance by delivering seven shutout innings in a 7–1 game 6 win that boosted his postseason record with the Astros to 4–0, as he had won a pair of games in that season's divisional round against the Boston Red Sox.

Highlights of his game 6 performance demonstrate why Verlander won the 2017 ALCS MVP award.

HELPS ASTROS WIN 2017 WORLD SERIES

Justin Verlander's first two trips to the World Series—in 2006 and 2012 with the Detroit Tigers—resulted in crushing losses to the St. Louis Cardinals and San Francisco Giants and long winter months filled with discontent. In 2017 with Houston, the ending was much different and far sweeter, as the Astros defeated the Los Angeles Dodgers in a seven-game thriller for the team's first title in franchise history. Verlander didn't collect a win in the series, but he was a prominent factor. In game 2, he pitched six innings and gave up only two hits in a game the Astros would eventually win 7–6 in 11 innings and, in game 6, held the potent Los Angeles lineup to two runs on three hits while striking out nine in a game the Astros would lose 3–1. The late-season acquisition of Verlander tilted the balance of power in the American League, fueled Houston's championship run, and fulfilled Verlander's dream of being a world champion.

Justin Verlander helped the Houston Astros win the 2017 World Series, and he joins the FOX MLB crew to talk about it.

season, then go 2–0 in the American League Championship Series with a ridiculous 0.56 earned run average (ERA). on his way to snagging ALCS MVP honors and then help the Astros win their first-ever World Series.

The eight-time All-Star won his 200th game and notched his 2,500th strikeout during the 2018 season. In 2019, still dealing nasty and mostly unhittable heat at the age of

Verlander lost two World Series with the Tigers before winning one in Houston.

thirty-six, Verlander threw an **unfathomable** third no-hitter of his career. The only pitchers to throw more in the history of the game were the Hall of Famers Nolan Ryan and Sandy Koufax.

Before the 2019 season began, Verlander signed a record-breaking $66 million contract extension to stay in Houston through the 2021 season. He is poised to add to his growing pile of wins and strikeouts, while continuing to push his way to the front of the line for entry into the Hall of Fame.

2. In what year did Justin Verlander reach the 2,500-strikeout milestone? Who did he record the strikeout against?

3. What did Justin Verlander do during the 2011 season that had been done only nine times prior in baseball history?

 RESEARCH PROJECT

Choose your favorite Major League Baseball team, and select an all-time best lineup. You can choose only one player at each position, so there are bound to be lots of difficult decisions, especially at pitcher, because you can pick only one starter and one reliever. Put together a colorful display with photos and statistics that highlight your all-time greats and prove that they deserve the honor.

WORDS TO UNDERSTAND

burgeoning: beginning to grow or increase rapidly; flourishing

covet: yearn to possess or have something

douse: extinguish; put out; smother

stingy: unwilling to give; ungenerous; tight

THE ROAD TO THE TOP

MAKING A SPLASH

The first clue that nine-year-old Justin Verlander and his right arm might be something special didn't materialize as one might suspect. Rather than firing fastballs past overmatched and inexperienced kids in a Saturday morning Little League game, his talent emerged in front of a pond at a park in Richmond, Virginia. It was at Deep Run Park, a scenic 160-plus-acre complex in western Henrico County, where the youngster's arm flashed power. While strolling the grounds, Verlander and his parents, Richard and Kathy, paused to do what all kids love to do at that age: throw rocks into the water. Richard launched one as far as he could and then watched in astonishment as Justin's throw sailed past his by a stunning margin. It was a defining moment in the early steps on the youngster's path to pitching greatness, and his parents would later write a book on raising athletic children that captured the importance of that park venture by titling it *Rocks Across the Pond*.

Despite the powerful arm, his parents stressed balance and variety, so Justin led an activity-filled childhood and sidestepped overuse injuries that

Verlander's throwing skills first came to his parents' attention when they noticed how far he could skip stones across a pond.

sabotage so many youngsters who are funneled into year-round play at early ages. There was basketball, church, and Cub Scouts among the pastimes, but it was the baseball diamond that yanked at his heart the hardest. By the time he was 10, he was devouring the insights of Bob Bralley, one of the most respected baseball instructors in the state, in one-on-one pitching sessions. Bralley spent several years in the New York Mets minor league system as a pitcher, served as a minor league manager and professional scout, and later became a legendary baseball coach at Highland Springs High School, which just happened to be a 45-minute drive from the Verlander home.

AN EYE ON EXCELLENCE

Verlander dove into the pursuit of becoming a great pitcher, and the result of the time and energy he devoted to the craft was slowly revealed in the ensuing years. He played on travel teams during his early teen years, where he was clocking mid-70s miles per hour on the radar gun. By the time he entered Goochland High School, more indicators of his **burgeoning** skill set emerged. Verlander overpowered hitters in his first outing on the junior varsity squad and was quickly elevated to the varsity, where he spent the remainder of his high school baseball career.

By the time Verlander's junior year rolled around, major league scouts were showing up regularly at his games, armed with their notebooks and radar guns. Routinely seeing pitches climb into the 90s, their interest was building. During the next 12 months Verlander appeared on track to face a difficult decision: whether to attend the college of his choice—he was being heavily recruited—or to be drafted by a major league team and head to the minor leagues as a teenager.

DRAFT DAY

During his senior year Verlander battled strep throat, which zapped the velocity on his pitches and **doused** some of the earlier interest shown by scouts. That illness, coupled with his parents letting major league teams know that if he was selected in the late rounds of the 2002 MLB draft he would head to college instead, steered teams away from spending a draft pick on him. His name was never called on draft day, so he opted to accept a baseball scholarship to Old Dominion University in Norfolk, Virginia. He had visited the campus and fell in love with the place, and during the three years he spent there Verlander shredded the record books.

Verlander attended Old Dominion University in Norfolk, Virginia, just a couple of hours from where he grew up.

MIGHTY MONARCH

Teams throughout the Colonial Athletic Association (CAA) would soon wish Verlander would have been drafted instead of choosing to pitch for the Old Dominion Monarchs, because he was dominant in his freshman season. He struck out 137 batters in 113.2 innings, with a stingy 1.90 ERA, on his way to being named the CAA Rookie of the Year. He completed eight of his 15 starts, struck out 10 or more batters on five occasions, and fanned a school record 17 hitters against James Madison University. Collegiate Baseball and Baseball America both named him a Freshman All-American.

Verlander's sophomore season was just as splendid as he continued racking up strikeouts, leading the CAA with 139 of them in 116.1 innings, which was also a single-season record for Old Dominion. He struck out 10 or more batters six times among his 15 starts and pocketed some impressive wins over traditional collegiate baseball powers along the way, including a 2–0 shutout of Vanderbilt and a 2–1 victory against Oklahoma State. He was also named an All-CAA First Team selection.

A glimpse of some of Justin Verlander's top moments on the mound throughout his career.

SUPER SUMMER

Verlander was chosen to be on Team USA, which competed at the 2003 Pan American Games in Santo Domingo, Dominican Republic. The team featured top collegiate baseball players from around the country, including future major league stars Dustin Pedroia and Jered Weaver.

In the lead-up to the games, the U.S. squad played a 22-game schedule, winning them all. Verlander got the starting nod to kick off the trip in Tucson, Arizona, as he struck out 10 over six innings of work while surrendering just one run as Team USA beat an Arizona team comprised of junior college All-Stars 3–1. Verlander was equally good a week later in Myrtle Beach, South Carolina, as he pitched 6.2 shutout innings with five strikeouts as Team USA silenced Japan 3–0.

WEARS RED, WHITE, AND BLUE AND WINS SILVER

When the Pan American Games commenced in early August, the U.S. team opened with shutout wins against Guatemala, the Bahamas, and the Dominican Republic. Its only loss in pool play came in a 3–0 setback against Nicaragua, which would be Verlander's only loss that summer. He was unable

Verlander played his college home games at the Bud Metheny Baseball Complex on campus.

to get through four innings in this outing, giving up all three runs (one of them unearned) on six hits and three walks. For the summer he finished with a 5–1 record and 1.34 ERA. He had 41 strikeouts in 40.1 innings. Verlander and his teammates brought home silver medals, as they defeated Mexico 3–2 in the semifinals but lost the gold medal game to Cuba 3–1.

CLOSING OUT COLLEGE CAREER

Verlander returned to Norfolk for his junior season, where his power and arsenal of pitches continued handcuffing opposing teams. He set new single-season CAA and ODU records for strikeouts with 151 of them in just 105.2 innings of work. His career mark of 427 strikeouts ranks first all-time in both Old Dominion and CAA history. He recorded double-digit strikeouts seven times among his 16 starts, including 17 against James Madison and 16 against Virginia Commonwealth. Verlander also picked up a win against nationally ranked Virginia. He ranked third in the nation in strikeouts per nine innings (12.8) and boasted a career strikeout average of 11.4 per nine innings. He was an easy choice for First Team All-CAA, and the Old Dominion Alumni Association named him the school's Male Athlete of the Year.

ARMED AND READY FOR THE PROS

Verlander's three seasons at Old Dominion, which were crammed with records and awards, attracted plenty of attention. Scouts from multiple major league teams showed up at games to size up the righty, who since his lanky high school days had packed on more than 30 pounds to fill out

EYE ON THE ESPYS

One of the biggest evenings on the sports calendar is the night in July when the ESPY Awards are given out. These are sports network ESPN's version of the Academy Awards in which individual and team achievements, as well as displays of courage and grace, are honored. In 2012, Justin Verlander was a finalist for two of these coveted awards: Best Male Athlete and Best Major League Baseball Player. He didn't win either category—LeBron James took home the Best Male Athlete Award, and Texas' Josh Hamilton won the Best MLB Player. Six years later, at the Microsoft Theater in Los Angeles, Verlander and his Houston teammates could add an ESPY to their World Series title as they won the Best Team award. They beat a powerful cast of nominees that included the Super Bowl champion Philadelphia Eagles and NBA champion Golden State Warriors.

his frame. Verlander had also improved his control, an issue that had raised some concern in the past. Coupled with his strong performance with Team USA, scouts were enthused about what they were seeing on the mound—and the big numbers sprouting on their radar guns, too—which shot his name to the top of many teams' list of players who were **coveted**.

On June 7, family and friends gathered at the Verlanders' two-story home for the 2004 Major League Baseball draft. In those days the draft wasn't televised. While Justin's dad was trying to complete the internet dial-up connection—an often slow and frustrating process—to follow along online, the phone in the Verlander home rang. On the other end of the line was Detroit Tigers General Manager Dave Dombrowski with some life-changing news: They were using their first pick (the second overall pick in the draft) to take Verlander.

STELLAR IN THE SUNSHINE

Verlander was assigned to the Lakeland Flying Tigers of the Florida State League, which features teams at the high end of the Class-A level. He certainly lived up to expectations as he posted a 9–2 record and 1.67 ERA in 13 starts. Verlander collected 104 strikeouts in 86 innings, while giving up 70 hits, 16 earned runs, three home runs, and 19 walks.

Verlander was promoted to the Erie SeaWolves of the Class-AA Eastern League, where he started seven games. He went 2–0 with a microscopic 0.20 ERA, as he gave up just one earned run in 32.2 innings while striking out 32.

In 2005, Verlander threw 32 innings for Erie of the Class-AA Eastern League, nicknamed, as the mascot clearly represents, the SeaWolves.

JUSTIN VERLANDER DRAFT DAY

- No lights, no cameras, no action: The two-day 2004 MLB draft was conducted via conference call with representatives of the league's 30 teams.

- The San Diego Padres selected shortstop Matt Bush, from Mission Bay High School in California, with the first pick.

- Righties from Rice: Three right-handed pitchers from Rice University (Philip Humber, Jeff Niemann, and Wade Townsend) were chosen among the first eight picks, the first time three players from the same university were chosen in the top 10 picks.

2004 MLB DRAFT
SIGNIFICANT ACCOUNTS

- Five future All-Stars were chosen in the first round: pitchers Justin Verlander, Jered Weaver, Glen Perkins, and Phil Hughes and third baseman Billy Butler.

- Three pitchers taken in the first round—Philip Humber (third), Homer Bailey (seventh), and Jered Weaver (12th)—threw no-hitters during the 2012 season. The White Sox's Humber's was a perfect game against Seattle.

- A flurry of firsts: Arizona State shortstop Dustin Pedroia, drafted by Boston in the second round (65th overall), was the first 2004 draftee to start an All-Star Game, the first to win a World Series, and the first to win a League MVP award.

- USC quarterback Matt Cassel was selected in the 36th round by Oakland but didn't sign and later played in the National Football League (NFL), most notably as Tom Brady's backup in New England.

- Former NFL quarterback Brian Brohm, the quarterback coach at Purdue University, was chosen in the 49th round by Colorado but didn't sign.

- Pitcher Nick Adenhart, taken by Anaheim in the 14th round, was killed in a car accident by a drunk driver after making his first start of the 2009 season.

- Dallas Braden, chosen 727th overall by Oakland, pitched the 19th perfect game in major league history in 2010 against Tampa Bay.

FIREWORKS ON THE FOURTH

The Fourth of July will always mean something extra special for Verlander. It was on this date in 2005 that he was called up from Erie to make his major league debut against the Indians at Jacobs Field in Cleveland in the second game of a doubleheader. He went 5.1 innings, giving up four runs on seven hits in the loss, and was optioned back to Erie.

Verlander was called up again less than three weeks later to once again start the second game of a doubleheader, this time at Comerica Park in Detroit against the Minnesota Twins. He gave up five runs on eight hits in six innings to take the loss. He returned to Erie, where he spent the remainder of the season.

Verlander's second career MLB start was his first at his home field, Comerica Park in Detroit.

TEXT-DEPENDENT QUESTIONS

1. What well-known coach did Justin Verlander receive personal instruction from during his youth? What was the man's background in baseball?

2. How many seasons did Verlander play at Old Dominion University? In which season did he record the most strikeouts?

3. What was Verlander's record for Team USA during the summer of 2003? How did Team USA fare at the Pan American Games?

RESEARCH PROJECT

Justin Verlander won 21 games and had 427 strikeouts in 335.2 innings during his three seasons at Old Dominion University. Can you find a pitcher who you can argue put up better numbers than Verlander in college during any three-year span?

WORDS TO UNDERSTAND

buoy: support; uplift

rejuvenate: to restore to an original or new state

ruthless: having or showing no pity or compassion for others

ON THE DIAMOND

MAGNIFICENT ON THE MOUND

When the Detroit Tigers used their second overall pick in the 2004 Major League Baseball draft on Justin Verlander, they hoped the hard-throwing righty from Old Dominion University would be a building block in the long journey ahead to restoring respectability to a franchise that had stumbled into hard times. But no one could have imagined *this* happening: mired in a 12-year stretch of losing seasons, Verlander was a force in resuscitating the Tigers and sparking hope in the Motor City. He fired fastballs and stacked up wins early and had a 7–3 record just two months into his rookie season. He finished with 17 wins, which was tied for most on the Detroit staff, and was handed the American League Rookie of the Year award. Plus, he helped the Tigers win 95 games, a remarkable transformation for a team that just three seasons earlier went 43–119. He also was a big factor in the Tigers going on to win two playoff series and play in the World Series (losing to the St. Louis Cardinals). Verlander's presence in the Tigers' starting rotation **rejuvenated** the fan base, helped propel them to another World Series appearance in 2012 (losing to the San Francisco Giants), and stamped him as one of the game's great pitchers.

DOMINANT IN DETROIT

Verlander pitched nearly 13 high-quality seasons in Detroit before being traded to Houston, putting his name throughout the Tigers' record books. He made nine opening day starts during his time in Motown, including a stretch of seven straight, which ranks him number 2 on the all-time Tigers' list behind

Verlander threw 2,373 strikeouts in his time with the Tigers.

Jack Morris's 11 straight starts. The 2,373 strikeouts he recorded are second all-time only to Mickey Lolich's 2,679. Verlander is seventh all-time in franchise wins with 183, whereas in strikeouts per nine innings, his 8.5 resides at third behind Max Scherzer (9.6), who is now with Washington, and Matthew Boyd (8.7). Verlander started 380 games for the Tigers, which is fifth all-time (Lolich leads at 459), and he is eighth in innings pitched at 2,511 (George Mullin is first at 3,394).

JUSTIN VERLANDER
Houston Astros
CAREER STATS

GP	GS	Wins	Losses	ERA	SO	BB
453	453	225	129	3.33	3006	850

PITCHER

- Date of birth: February 20, 1983

- Height: six feet five inches (1.96 meters)

- Selected second overall by the Detroit Tigers in the 2004 MLB draft

- World Series Champion (2017)

- American League Rookie of the Year (2006)

- Eight All-Star Game appearances (started for American League in 2019 and 2012)

- Two-time American League Cy Young Award winner (2011, 2019)

- American League Most Valuable Player (2011)

- American League Championship Series MVP (2017)

- Led major leagues in wins three times (2009, 2011, and 2019)

SUPERSTITIOUS SACRIFICE

Baseball players are generally some of the most superstitious athletes in all of sports. So when their team's pitcher has a no-hitter going, there are some key rules to follow: No one mentions the words "no-hitter," no one talks to the pitcher in the dugout, and everyone repeats where they sat and what they did in the dugout the previous inning. When Justin Verlander was in the midst of throwing a no-hitter in 2011 against Toronto, his catcher Alex Avila had to use the restroom after the sixth inning. But Avila knew that doing so could disrupt the good vibes swirling around the Detroit dugout, so he fought off the urge for the sake of his team. Once Verlander had secured the no-hitter and the Tigers had celebrated with high-fives, hugs, and dumping a cooler of water on the ace pitcher, Avila quickly found his way to the restroom.

Verlander won 15 or more games for Detroit eight times and gobbled up big innings virtually every season. He was remarkably healthy considering the load he carried. Prior to the 2014 season, Verlander had core muscle surgery to repair an abdominal injury that flared up while he was performing offseason conditioning drills, but he still managed to pitch more than 200 innings and win 15 games that season. In 2015, he spent the first couple of months of the season on the disabled list due to problems with his triceps and back, which limited him to 20 starts, the fewest of his major league career. But the following season Verlander returned to the form that Detroit fans had become accustomed to and opposing hitters dreaded, as he led the American League in strikeouts and won 16 games.

HELLO HOUSTON

The Astros acquired Verlander in the closing minutes of the trade deadline on August 31, 2017, and five days later he made his debut in

Verlander joined his new teammates with Houston during the stretch run for the 2017 playoffs.

a 3–1 win against Seattle at Safeco Field. He struck out seven in six innings of work, the lone blemish on his 103-pitch evening coming on Kyle Seager's full-count home run in the fourth inning. For the record, Verlander's first pitch as an Astro was a ball to Jean Segura, and his first strikeout victim was Robinson Cano. A week later he was on the mound in Anaheim, delivering a performance that had the Astros' fan base salivating for the postseason. Verlander gave up a leadoff double to Brandon Phillips, and then no other Angel reached base via a hit over the eight shutdown innings he threw in the 1–0 win.

On September 17, more than 30,000 fans showed up at Minute Maid Park on a Sunday afternoon to check out Verlander's home debut against Seattle. He won his third start in a row, giving up just one run in seven innings while striking out 10 in the 7–1 win that also secured Houston's first American League West division championship. Verlander also won his final two starts of the regular season to finish with a perfect 5–0 mark and 1.06 ERA, and he was clearly ready to lead the Astros into the playoffs. Here is a closer look at Verlander's regular season production:

Year	Team	W	L	ERA	GS	CG	IP	H	HR	BB	SO
2005	DET	0	2	7.15	2	0	11.1	15	1	5	7
2006	DET	17	9	3.63	30	1	186.0	187	21	60	124
2007	DET	18	6	3.66	32	1	201.2	181	20	67	183
2008	DET	11	*17*	4.84	33	1	201.0	195	18	87	163
2009	DET	*19*	9	3.45	*35*	3	*240.0*	219	20	63	*269*
2010	DET	18	9	3.37	33	4	224.1	190	14	71	219
2011	DET	*24*	5	**2.40**	*34*	4	*251.0*	174	24	57	*250*
2012	DET	17	8	2.64	33	*6*	*238.1*	192	19	60	*239*
2013	DET	13	12	3.46	*34*	0	218.1	212	19	75	217
2014	DET	15	12	4.54	32	0	206.0	223	18	65	159
2015	DET	5	8	3.38	20	1	133.1	113	13	32	113
2016	DET	16	9	3.04	34	2	227.2	171	30	57	*254*
2017	DET	10	8	3.82	28	0	172.0	153	23	67	176
2017	HOU	5	0	1.06	5	0	34.0	17	4	5	43
2018	HOU	16	9	2.52	*34*	1	214.0	156	28	37	*290*
2019	HOU	*21*	6	2.58	34	2	*223.0*	137	36	42	300
Total		225	129	3.33	453	26	2,982.0	2,535	308	850	3,006

Bold: indicates season totals led the American League; *Italic:* indicates season totals led the major leagues

Verlander's regular season success has allowed him to be selected to appear in eight career All-Star Games.

POSTSEASON PERFORMER

Houston's march through the 2017 postseason was **buoyed** by the addition of Verlander, who dazzled. He opened game 1 of the American League Division Series by holding Boston to two runs in Houston's 8–2 drubbing and picked up the win in relief of Charlie Morton in game 4's series-clinching 5–4 win. In the American League Championship Series against New York Verlander was **ruthless** as he silenced a lethal lineup that had won 91 games during the regular season. He won both games he pitched, giving up just one run in 16 innings, and claimed the ALCS MVP award. In the World Series, Verlander was not as sharp, going 0–1 in two starts. The Astros, however, won the series in seven games.

Back in 2012, Verlander had a similar streak of spectacular pitching for Detroit, as he won two games against Oakland in the divisional series while racking up 22 strikeouts. He opened game 1 with a three-hit, one-run win

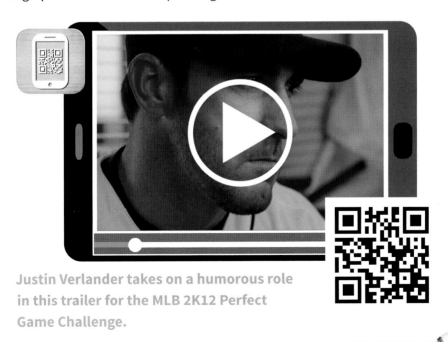

Justin Verlander takes on a humorous role in this trailer for the MLB 2K12 Perfect Game Challenge.

and shut out the A's in a four-hit series clincher in game 5. Verlander ran his postseason record that year to 3–0, when he collected the game 3 win against New York by allowing just one Yankee to cross the plate.

Verlander has appeared in a total of three World Series, starting five games, but he hasn't earned a win yet. Here is a closer look at his pitching in the pressure-filled playoffs:

Year	Team	Series	Rslt	Opp	W	L	ERA	GS	CG	IP	H	ER	HR	BB	SO
2006	DET	ALDS	W	NYY	0	0	5.06	1	0	5.1	7	3	1	4	5
2006	DET	ALCS	W	OAK	1	0	6.75	1	0	5.1	7	4	2	1	6
2006	DET	WS	L	STL	0	2	5.73	2	0	11.0	12	7	2	5	12
2011	DET	ALDS	W	NYY	1	0	5.00	2	0	9.0	6	5	0	5	12
2011	DET	ALCS	L	TEX	1	1	5.56	2	0	11.1	13	7	2	5	13
2012	DET	ALDS	W	OAK	2	0	0.56	2	1	16.0	7	1	1	5	22
2012	DET	ALCS	W	NYY	1	0	1.08	1	0	8.1	3	1	1	0	3
2012	DET	WS	L	SFG	0	1	11.25	1	0	4.0	6	5	2	1	4
2013	DET	ALDS	W	OAK	1	0	0.00	2	0	15.0	6	0	0	2	21
2013	DET	ALCS	L	BOS	0	1	1.13	1	0	8.0	4	1	1	1	10
2014	DET	ALDS	L	BAL	0	0	5.40	1	0	5.0	6	3	1	1	4
2017	HOU	ALDS	W	BOS	2	0	3.12	1	0	8.2	7	3	1	4	3
2017	HOU	ALCS	W	NYY	2	0	0.56	2	1	16	10	1	0	2	21
2017	HOU	WS	W	LAD	0	1	3.75	2	0	12.0	5	5	2	2	14
2018	HOU	ALDS	W	CLE	1	0	3.38	1	0	5.1	2	2	0	2	7
2018	HOU	ALCS	L	BOS	1	1	4.50	2	0	12.0	9	6	2	6	10
2019	HOU	ALDS	W	TBR	1	1	3.38	2	0	10.2	8	4	2	6	13
2019	HOU	ALCS	W	NYY	0	1	3.95	2	0	13.2	10	6	3	2	16
2019	HOU	WS	L	WSN	0	2	5.73	2	0	11.0	12	7	3	6	9
TOTALS					14	11	3.40	31	30	187.2	140	71	26	60	205
7 ALDS					7	0	2.38	11	1	64.1	41	17	4	23	74
6 ALCS					6	3	2.95	9	1	61.0	46	20	8	15	63
3 WS					0	4	5.67	5	0	27.0	23	17	6	8	30

OTHER CAREER HIGHLIGHTS

Here are some additional highlights from Verlander's career:

- Led major leagues in games started in 2009 (35), 2011 (34), and 2013 (34)
- Led major leagues in innings pitched in 2009 (240.0), 2011 (251.0), 2012 (238.1), and 2019 (224)
- 2011 American League Triple Crown (24–5, 2.40 ERA, 250 strikeouts)
- The *Sporting News* Major League Player of the Year (2011)
- Started for the Astros on opening day of the 2019 season at Tampa Bay, his 11th career opening day start
- Became the fifth pitcher in MLB history to record 290 or more strikeouts at age thirty-five or older
- Led major leagues in strikeouts three times (2012, 2011, and 2009)
- Led American League in ERA in 2011 (2.40)
- Joined Roger Clemens (2004) as the only pitchers to start their careers with the Astros on a nine-game regular season winning streak
- Had a career-long 12-game winning streak during the 2011 season with Detroit

When NY Yankee lefthander CC Sabathia retired after the 2019 season, Verlander became the active leader in career wins and strikeouts. Sabathia averaged 13 wins a season compared to Verlander's 15.

COMPARISON WITH CONTEMPORARIES

Verlander's numbers match up very well with pitching greats of his era. The Yankees' CC Sabathia entered the league five seasons before Verlander, so he joined the 250-win club and recorded his 3,000th strikeout before Verlander hit 3,000 Ks in 2019. Verlander will hit 250 wins sometime in 2021 if he stays healthy. Both pitchers have won the Cy Young Award—Sabathia in 2007—and each has led the American League in wins, Sabathia twice and Verlander three times, though Verlander's career season-high 24 victories is higher than Sabathia's season-best 21.

LA's Clayton Kershaw is the only active pitcher other than Verlander to have won both a Cy Young Award and a league MVP award in the same season.

In the National League the Dodgers' Clayton Kershaw pulled off the same rare double in 2014 that Verlander did in 2011 by winning both the Cy Young Award and his league's MVP award. Kershaw's numbers were out of this world: 21–3 with a 1.77 ERA and six complete games. The Dodgers' lefty has won a total of three Cy Young Awards.

TEXT-DEPENDENT QUESTIONS

1. In what year did Justin Verlander win his first Cy Young Award? What other prestigious award did he claim that season?

2. Who did Verlander face in his home debut for the Houston Astros? What else was significant about that game?

3. What postseason award did Verlander earn with Houston in 2017?

RESEARCH PROJECT

Justin Verlander has been spectacular in the ALDS and ALCS, going a combined 13–3 with Detroit and Houston, but in the World Series, he is 0–4. Compile a list of the top pitchers in the history of baseball who were dominant in the regular season and postseason but never won a game in the World Series.

WORDS TO UNDERSTAND

allude: suggest or call attention to indirectly; hint at; mention witho[ut] discussing at length

cauldron: something resembling a large pot (cauldron) boiling in intensity or degree of agitation

extricate: free someone or something from a constraint or difficult[y]

veil: something that hides or obscures like a cover of cloth (veil)

CHAPTER 4

WORDS COUNT

When the time comes to address the media before or after a game, players either retreat to the comfort of traditional phrases that avoid controversy (Cliché City), or they speak their mind with refreshing candor (Quote Machine).

Here are 10 quotes, compiled in part from the website BrainyQuote.com, with some insight as to the context of what Justin Verlander is talking about or referencing:

"I knew it was different than a regular in-season game. I didn't know what to expect, really. Walking in from the bullpen, I'm usually pretty focused and in my zone. They started playing the tribute video, and I couldn't help but stop and look at it and just take a minute and just be out there with the fans and appreciate some moments that we shared together the last 13 years."

When Houston visited Detroit for a three-game series near the end of the 2018 season, it had been 375 days since the Tigers had traded Verlander to the Astros. When he stepped on the field at Comerica Park to prepare to face his former team, a **cauldron** of emotions was simmering. Heading from his warm-up session in the bullpen to the dugout, a tribute video highlighting his years in the Motor City played on the giant scoreboard in left field, hijacking his pregame focus. He couldn't help but enjoy the look back at some wonderful years in a city that embraced him from the start. But, once he dug his cleats into the pitcher's mound in the bottom of the first inning, he put the brakes on the trip down memory lane and went to work. He went seven innings—bookended by strikeouts of Jeimer Candelario to start the first and finish the seventh—to earn a 3–2 win. **Rating: Quote Machine**

> "I'd be lying if I said I didn't know the list of guys who've thrown three instead of two gets pretty small. Some of the guys I idolize. It's a special moment."

Verlander has fond memories of the 13 seasons he spent in Detroit.

JUSTIN VERLANDER

NUMBER 35 JERSEY RETIRED

Justin Verlander is the greatest pitcher in Old Dominion University history, so it was only fitting that he became the first baseball player there to have his jersey retired. He pitched for the Monarchs from 2002 to 2004, where he won 21 games and recorded 427 strikeouts in just 335.2 innings. His number 35 jersey was retired during a special ceremony at the Ted Constant Convocation Center on campus in 2010 during a basketball game between Georgetown and the Monarchs. An image of Verlander is on the outfield fence padding at the Bud Metheny Complex where the Old Dominion baseball team plays.

When Verlander induced Toronto rookie Bo Bichette to ground out to third in the bottom of the ninth inning on the first day of September during the 2019 season, he secured his third career no-hitter. The extraordinary feat took him into sacred terrain, which Verlander **alluded** to in his postgame comments amid the celebration of his tying Cy Young, Bob Feller, and Larry Corcoran at number three on the all-time list. Plus, this was Verlander's second no-hitter against the Blue Jays in Toronto, earning him the distinction of being the only pitcher to ever throw two no-hitters as a visitor in the same ballpark. He threw his first no-hitter against Toronto on May 7, 2011, and got the first of his career four years earlier in Detroit against Milwaukee. On the all-time no-hitter list Verlander trails only Nolan Ryan with seven and Sandy Koufax with four.

Rating: Quote Machine

"**That's one thing that I wish could change from the past. I felt bad because Mr. I put his heart and soul into this organization and did everything he possibly could to allow us to win a championship, and we came close a couple times. Probably one of my biggest regrets is not winning one for him.**"

One of the most beloved figures in Detroit during Verlander's time there was Mike Ilitch, owner of both the Detroit Tigers and Detroit Red Wings, who was affectionately known as Mr. I. He founded Little Caesars Pizza and was a driving force behind the city's downtown rebirth. The Red Wings won four Stanley Cups under his ownership, but the Tigers—while coming close—weren't able to get Mr. I a World Series title that he so craved. In 2006, the Tigers lost in the World Series to the St. Louis Cardinals 4–1 in the

Verlander and catcher Alex Avila pose for a photograph with Tiger's owner Mike Ilitch.

best-of-seven series. Verlander didn't pitch as well as he would have liked, taking the losses in games 1 and 5, where he gave up a combined seven earned runs in 11 innings of work. Six years later Detroit had another chance but were swept by San Francisco. Mr. I passed away in 2017. **Rating: Quote Machine**

> "I'm more of a feel pitcher. If something's wrong, I don't watch a video. I go throw in the bullpen until it feels right."

Major League pitchers choose lots of different routes for **extricating** themselves from rocky patches during the long season. Some consume hours of video, dissecting footage with their pitching coaches of what they are doing wrong on the mound, or even revisiting older tape of when they were dialed

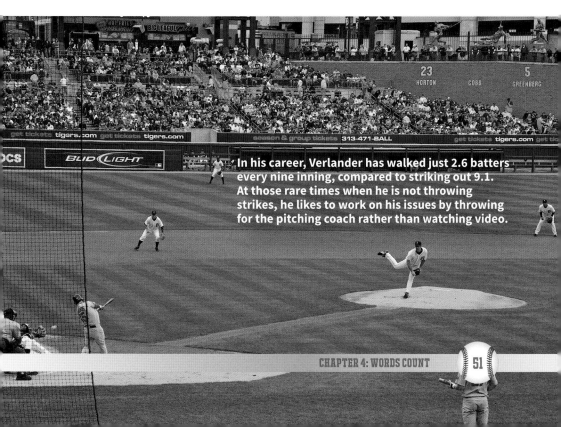

In his career, Verlander has walked just 2.6 batters every nine inning, compared to striking out 9.1. At those rare times when he is not throwing strikes, he likes to work on his issues by throwing for the pitching coach rather than watching video.

in that is used to spark positive images that they can take with them into the next game. Verlander prefers to iron out any problems that arise by working up a sweat. By throwing on the mound in the solitude of the bullpen, under the watchful eyes of the club's pitching coach, he can tinker with everything, from his body positioning to his release point, and resolve the problem. This leads to big problems for hitters. **Rating: Quote Machine**

"I tell you, man, it really made me feel special. It makes you feel so embraced, seeing everybody, seeing how excited they were when I met them face-to-face. To hear and feel and see that emotion before I'm even here, man. It made me feel so much more comfortable coming into a scary situation, really. This is so unique, so different, a first-day-of-school feeling."

As news that the Houston Astros had acquired Justin Verlander at the 2017 trade deadline snaked its way throughout the lineup, the reactions that the All-Star pitcher heard about the deal helped make the transition to a new team a smooth one. Once he met his new team in Seattle, where they were kicking off a 10-game West Coast swing, walking into the visitors' clubhouse at Safeco Field wasn't quite as unnerving as those first-day-with-a-new-team jitters tend to be. There were lots of celebratory reactions to adding Verlander's potent right arm for their postseason push, including that of shortstop Carlos Correa, who upon hearing the news sent his PlayStation 4 remote control airborne, too excited to remember to catch it as it crashed to the floor and broke. Outfielder George Springer screamed when he read a text message about Verlander's acquisition. **Rating: Quote Machine**

News that Verlander (R) was an Astro thrilled his new teammates in 2017.

"**I can't even put it into words. The experience is everything I dreamed it would be. But I didn't take a second of this for granted because having been here twice and falling short, I know how hard it is to win the World Series.**"

The list of Hall of Fame players who never won a World Series is long: Ernie Banks of the Chicago Cubs, Boston's Ted Williams, San Diego's Tony Gwynn, and San Francisco pitching great Juan Marichal, among so many others.

Verlander certainly didn't want to hear his name included in *that* conversation, but after two failed attempts with Detroit—they lost the 2006 and 2012 World Series—opportunities for winning one were diminishing as he reached his mid-thirties. So when he was able to play a prominent role in helping Houston win its first title in franchise history in 2017, he fulfilled a life-long dream and struggled to be original in describing what it meant to be a part of such a captivating march to a championship. **Rating: Cliché City**

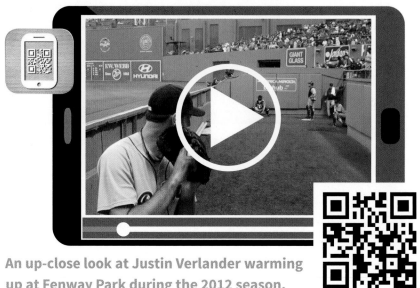

An up-close look at Justin Verlander warming up at Fenway Park during the 2012 season.

"**When I came into baseball, I had one goal for my career—the Hall of Fame.**"

When it comes to athletes and their career goals, there often is a **veil** of secrecy surrounding them. Many refuse to reveal their hopes and dreams in

Getting into the Baseball Hall of Fame has always been on Verlander's mind.

the sport to the media—opting instead for generic responses—since sharing for public consumption what they truly hope to achieve can result in endless questions and analysis as they navigate their careers. Verlander, however, was refreshingly candid in this response, as he has always possessed a fierce desire to be the best and isn't afraid to say it and then go out on the mound and back it up. When he left Detroit, he had 183 wins and more than 2,300 strikeouts, but because his résumé was missing a World Series title, his name was among many in that iffy category when it came to Hall of Fame worthiness. Since arriving in Houston, he has checked the World Series winner box and pushed himself into the Hall of Fame conversation.

Rating: Quote Machine

"Any time you get the opportunity to represent—not only yourself but your organization, the American League, Major League Baseball—it's such an honor. I don't take these games for granted."

Justin Verlander threw a grand total of 14 pitches during the 2019 All-Star Game, but each of them was meaningful and—unsurprisingly—unhittable. Verlander was chosen as the American League's starting pitcher for the Midsummer Classic at Progressive Field in Cleveland. With his 40th birthday lurking just four years away, he recognizes the importance of relishing these moments more than ever. Of course, he also wants to remain focused on the field and deliver for his teammates, which is exactly what he did on this evening.

In 2015, Dallas Keuchel became the fourth Astros pitcher to start an All-Star Game. Verlander was the fifth.

He got Christian Yelich to line out and then struck out Javier Baez and Freddie Freeman to close out his work for the evening. He was able to relax and enjoy this annual gathering of the greats before delivering this gem of a cliché. He became the fifth Houston Astro to start an All-Star Game, joining Dallas Keuchel (2015), Roger Clemens (2004), Mike Scott (1987), and J. R. Richard (1980). **Rating: Cliché City**

> **"If it was truly a baseball decision, it's a no brainer. It's an easy decision, but the way that that city has treated me since I got there and how I felt so connected to them is what made the decision so difficult."**

Verlander had about a half-hour before the trade deadline expired during the 2017 season to make a gigantic career decision: either waive his no-trade clause and be dealt to Houston or remain in Detroit where he had pitched for more than a decade. The Astros had great appeal because their talent-laden

It was a difficult decision for Verlander to give up his Detroit colors and agree to be traded to Houston in 2017.

roster was poised for a playoff run, while the Tigers were in the midst of dreadful rebuilding years. While Verlander's love for Detroit and the city tugged at his heart to stay (as he alludes to in the clichéd quote), he is a competitor who craves winning, and the Astros were in position to do a lot of it, which ultimately was the deciding factor as the deal was done with just minutes to spare. **Rating: Cliché City**

"**That's what I've learned over the years. It happened so quickly; you can forget about it so quickly. I took a minute to walk around the field and take it all in, look at the stadium. To be here, I feel like I need to do a little bit better job taking advantage of it. These guys are my new friends, my new family. This is what it's all about.**"

Justin Verlander had pitched in plenty of big games during his days in Detroit, but as his career has advanced to the latter stages, he's recognizing that those special moments of locking down a playoff spot after a grinding six-month season need to be savored more. So after making his home pitching debut at Minute Maid Park—a seven-inning gem to help the Astros clinch their first American League West Division title with a 7–1 win over Seattle—he spent extra time looking around the stadium as celebrations broke out throughout the stands and on the field with his new teammates. **Rating: Quote Machine**

TEXT-DEPENDENT QUESTIONS

1. How did Justin Verlander fare in his first game back in Detroit facing his old team? Who won the game?

2. What is one of Justin Verlander's biggest regrets from his time with the Detroit Tigers?

3. How many Houston Astros pitchers have started the All-Star Game in its history? Who are they?

RESEARCH PROJECT

The All-Star Game has produced many memorable moments through the years. Take a look back and put together your top 10 list of all-time great performances, and have enough supporting facts to back up your rankings.

WORDS TO UNDERSTAND

coffer: money box; a strongbox or small chest for holding valuables

nuances: subtle differences or distinctions

paparazzi: freelance photographers who pursue celebrities to get photographs of them

savvy: shrewd and knowledgeable; having common sense and good judgment

CHAPTER 5

OFF THE DIAMOND

HOUSTON AND HOLLYWOOD

Justin Verlander's life has all the makings of a Hollywood movie script, which certainly seems appropriate because one of the greatest pitchers in baseball history resides amid the glitz and glamour of Beverly Hills during the offseason with his supermodel, mega-star wife, Kate Upton. A 2017 World Series champion, proud new dad of a beautiful baby girl, and owner of a giant contract extension, Verlander's journey from a small town in Virginia to super stardom on the field, and one half of a celebrity couple followed by **paparazzi** off it, is stunning.

"I DO" IN ITALY

During the Houston Astros' World Series victory parade that wound through downtown in 2017 and culminated with a rally at City Hall with hundreds of thousands of fans lining the streets, one super-important member of the team who helped it secure the first title in franchise history was noticeably absent

Verlander married supermodel Kate Upton in 2017.

from the celebration: Justin Verlander. The Astros' ace had a good reason for missing the festivities—he was in Italy marrying supermodel and actress Kate Upton.

The two began dating in 2014, were engaged two years later, and got married in 2017, days after the Astros' World Series clincher, at a medieval church in Tuscany, Italy. They honeymooned in Puglia, known for its scenic Mediterranean coastline, in southern Italy.

The Verlanders are one of the most well-known celebrity couples in the world. They are often seen together at high-profile events and even made an appearance together on *The Tonight Show*. Upton has appeared on the cover of the *Sports Illustrated* swimsuit issue several times and was the subject of the 100th anniversary cover of *Vanity Fair*. She appeared on *Saturday Night Live* in 2012 and has had roles in several movies, including *The Layover*, *The Other Woman*, *The Three Stooges*, and *Tower Heist*. Upton also starred in the music video for Lady Antebellum's "Bartender" in 2014.

PROUD PARENTS

Verlander has enjoyed many special moments throughout his career, but his proudest arrived on November 7, 2018, with the birth of his daughter,

Genevieve Upton Verlander. He and his wife shared photos of her on their Instagram accounts. Justin posted a photo of his hand and Upton's hand holding

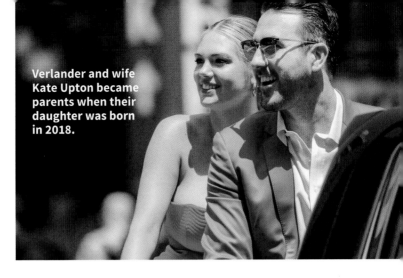

Verlander and wife Kate Upton became parents when their daughter was born in 2018.

Genevieve's hand, and Upton shared a photo of the baby sleeping.

OFF-SEASON COMFORT

Verlander and his family reside in Beverly Hills, California, during the offseason on a $5.25 million estate they purchased the year before they got married. The 5,706-square-foot home has a long history of well-known owners, which includes famous saxophonist Kenny G, 14-time Grand Slam tennis champion Pete Sampras, and original *Charlie's Angels* actress Kate Jackson. The gated home provides the privacy they desire to escape life in the public, and there is a pool, spa, tennis court, and several outdoor lounge areas spread throughout the 1½-acre property to relax and enjoy the California sunshine.

REPRESENTATION

Verlander is represented by agent Mark Pieper, the CEO at Independent Sports and Entertainment, a sports, media, entertainment, and management company that represents more than 300 baseball, football, and basketball players. Baseball players represented include slugger Miguel Cabrera,

BIG BILL

Houston Astros fans will never forget how valuable Justin Verlander was on the march to the 2017 World Series title—and apparently neither will fans of the Los Angeles Dodgers. The Astros defeated the Dodgers 4–3 in the best-of-seven series. When the Astros were in Los Angeles the following season for a series against the Angels, Verlander went out for breakfast at the Beverly Hills Hotel and received an expensive—and humorous—bill. Among the charges were a $9 latte with skim milk, a $10 cranberry juice, $30 pancakes, and a miscellaneous charge of $1 million for "Dodger Killer." Verlander enjoyed the staff's joke and later posted a photo of the bill on his Instagram account.

Verlander's former teammate in Detroit, as well as San Francisco Giants' pitcher Mark Melancon, and Cleveland Indians' manager Terry Francona.

HEFTY RAISE

During spring training of 2019, Verlander signed a record-breaking contract extension worth $66 million that will keep him in a Houston Astros uniform through the 2021 season. Without the deal, Verlander would have hit free agency during the 2019 offseason, where any team willing to dig deep into its **coffers** would have had the chance to sign him. The $33 million Verlander will receive in 2020 and 2021 is the highest annual salary for a pitcher in major league history, bettering the $32.5 million salary of Houston teammate Zack Greinke. (Greinke's six-year, $206.5 million deal includes some deferred money that is not included when calculating annual salary, whereas Verlander's deal has no deferred money written into the contract.)

Record contracts are nothing new to Verlander. During spring training in 2013, while pitching in Detroit, he agreed to what at that time was a record extension of $140 million that kicked in for the 2015 season and was expected to keep him in a Tigers' uniform through the 2019 season. Combined

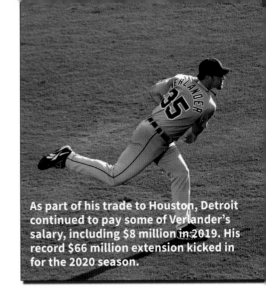

As part of his trade to Houston, Detroit continued to pay some of Verlander's salary, including $8 million in 2019. His record $66 million extension kicked in for the 2020 season.

with the $40 million the club already owed him for the 2013 and 2014 seasons, Verlander would pocket $180 million during the next seven seasons. Broken down, he was paid $20 million in 2013 and 2014 and then received a pay bump to $28 million per season beginning in 2015. At that time the deal was the biggest ever for a pitcher for average annual salary, edging out the seven-year, $175 million extension the Seattle Mariners gave Felix Hernandez.

NOTABLE NOTE

Major League Baseball scouts weren't the only ones who saw the talent oozing from Verlander during his high school days. Daniel Hicks, one of Verlander's best friends, loaned him 50 cents in the 10th grade to get a chocolate milk on one condition: he had Verlander sign a note agreeing to give Hicks 1/10 of 1 percent of

Seattle's Felix Hernandez was baseball's highest-paid pitcher until Verlander signed his last contract in Detroit in 2015.

his signing bonus. Hicks hung onto the note, and years later Verlander received a signing bonus from Detroit worth more than $3 million. When the two met to tee it up on the golf course, Hicks dug out the note and showed it to Verlander. The two had a good laugh, and Hicks told Verlander that he wasn't going to cash it in—that he might wait until the next bonus.

BASEBALL BROTHERHOOD

While Verlander was competing in youth baseball and on travel teams during his teen years, one of his biggest fans was his brother, Ben. Nine years younger than Verlander, Ben was at most of the games and developed a love for baseball, too. At Goochland High School he was a dominant pitcher and excellent hitter who went on to play at Old Dominion University like Justin. Ben converted from pitching to the outfield while playing for the Monarchs and was named a Third Team All-American. In 2013, he hit .367 with 11 home runs, and he tied a school record with a three-homer game against Northeastern. The Detroit Tigers drafted him in the 14th round in 2013 and assigned him to the Lakeland Flying Tigers in the Florida State League, the same team that Justin had begun his professional career with years earlier. Ben's best season in Lakeland was 2016, when he hit .252, with five home runs and 39 runs batted in (RBI) in 80 games. He eventually played a total of 421 games in the minors over a five-year career.

POSITIVE PARENTING

Richard and Kathy Verlander are proud parents of two sons, one who just so happens to be one of the greatest starting pitchers in MLB today. While

Justin Verlander and his wife Kate Upton appeared on *The Tonight Show* with Jimmy Fallon and shared their busy month of winning the World Series and getting married.

raising Verlander, and later his younger brother Ben, they stressed finding a child's passion—regardless of whether it's baseball, music, or another endeavor—and creating a plan to help them strive to pursue it. The two wrote a book about their parenting philosophies titled *Rocks Across the Pond*, which was published in 2012. It features details on many of Justin's life experiences and how he developed into a major league pitcher. The title comes from Richard throwing a rock into a pond when Justin was nine years old, and the youngster followed by sending a rock far beyond Richard's throw. That moment sent them on an odyssey of exploration.

Richard wasn't knowledgeable in the **nuances** of the game, so he headed to the library to get a book on pitching. He also enlisted a personal

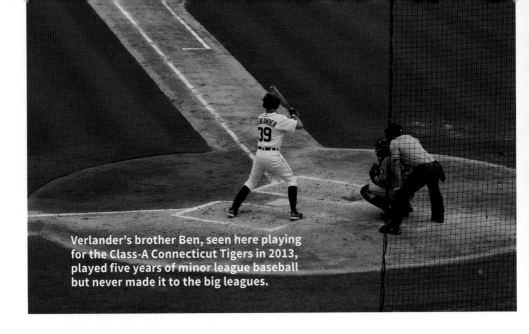

Verlander's brother Ben, seen here playing for the Class-A Connecticut Tigers in 2013, played five years of minor league baseball but never made it to the big leagues.

coach with a **savvy** baseball background to help teach proper pitching technique. Most important of all, perhaps, Verlander's parents preached diversity in his activities. He played different sports, including basketball on the high school team. This enabled him to rest his arm for several months of the year while he developed different muscles and movements from different activities that would bolster his pitching form.

Richard and Kathy have done numerous book signings, as well as given presentations to kids about following their dreams, doing something they love, and sharing their success and doing good for others. It's a terrific message that Justin has embraced, as evidenced by the charitable work he has been involved with through the years.

WINS FOR WARRIORS FOUNDATION

In 2016 Verlander created his Wins for Warriors Foundation, a charity aimed at empowering military veterans and raising awareness through innovative family-bonding activities. Verlander has spoken often about how thankful he is to have the freedom to continue living his dream of playing professional baseball, so he helps celebrate and honor those military members, veterans, and their families who have made enormous sacrifices for the country.

Verlander's Wins for Warriors Foundation supports nonprofit organizations that empower veterans.

HOSTS ANNUAL PATRIOT RUCK

Verlander hosts a unique annual event—the Patriot Ruck—along Detroit's riverfront to honor all military members, first responders, and veterans who have sacrificed and served since the 9/11 attacks in New York, Washington,

To honor the sacrifice of the military and first responders since the 9/11 attacks, Verlander hosts a charity event in Detroit every year.

DC, and Pennsylvania. The event is open to anyone, and participants are encouraged to walk either the three- or six-mile course with a weighted backpack (rucksack) to simulate the weight carried by first responders and the ruck marches required of all servicemen and women in the U.S. military. His third annual event was held in September of 2019 and attracted more than 1,000 participants. There are also family activities, food, music, and a special resource expo for veterans and military personnel.

GRAND SLAM ADOPTION EVENTS

Verlander and his wife love dogs—a lot. They have adopted dogs of their own and frequently visit animal shelters around the country. Upton has also volunteered at animal adoption shelters. So their annual Grand Slam Adoption Event has been a natural fit for the pair and a huge help to others.

Every year before a spring training game they host their event, which pairs a rescue dog that has been trained to become a service dog with a veteran, to help with his or her transition into civilian life. The Verlanders are using the healing power of animals to help veterans dealing with posttraumatic stress disorder adjust to their new lives. The annual event also promotes dog adoptions and illustrates the healing power of those special animal–human bonds.

HURRICANE HELP

Hurricane Harvey was a devastating Category 4 hurricane that inflicted mass destruction on parts of Texas and Louisiana in August of 2017. It caused horrific flooding, damage, and many deaths. It was the first major hurricane to make landfall in the United States since Wilma in 2005. Verlander was one of many notable individuals to lend support, as he donated his 2017 postseason check of $439,000 to help those affected.

TEXT-DEPENDENT QUESTIONS

1. Where did Justin Verlander marry Kate Upton? What significant event did he miss in Houston due to the wedding date?

2. What television show did the couple appear on together? What is a magazine cover Kate Upton has appeared on?

3. What is the name of the foundation that Justin Verlander created? Who is it aimed at helping? What are some of the events that it conducts?

RESEARCH PROJECT

Debate Duel: You and a friend each choose a Major League Baseball franchise that has never won a World Series: the list includes the Washington Nationals, Seattle Mariners, Texas Rangers, Colorado Rockies, Tampa Bay Rays, and Milwaukee Brewers. Each of you assumes the role of an agent that must convince a high-profile pitcher to drop his no-trade clause and come to the franchise you have chosen. Who can make the best case? Things to consider while putting together your argument are the team's current roster, winning potential in the next few years, how much money the team has available to spend on free agents, the stability of the ownership, and whether they have a long-term manager in place.

All-Star: a player chosen by fans and managers to play on the All-Star team against the opposing league in the MLB All-Star game in the middle of the season. The league that wins hosts the first game of the World Series.

box: the rectangle where the batter stands or the area where the pitcher fields the ball; also called the batter's box.

breaking ball: any pitch that curves in the air: a curve ball, slider, screwball, sinker, or forkball.

bunt: a ball batted for a short distance to help the batter to reach first base or to advance another runner on base while the defense makes the out at first.

change-up: a slow pitch that throws off a batter's timing.

cleanup: the fourth hitter in the lineup, usually the best hitter on the team. If all three runners get on base before the cleanup hitter, it's up to him to get them home, likely with a home run.

closer: the pitcher called in during the last innings to preserve a lead.

curve: a pitch that spins the ball with a snap of the wrist, forcing it to curve near the plate.

Cy Young Award: the award given annually to the pitcher in each of the American and National Leagues deemed to be the most outstanding in the regular season. The award winner is determined by votes cast by the Baseball Writers' Association of America, a professional association for baseball journalists.

designated hitter (DH): the player who hits for the pitcher. This position was created in 1973 and is used only in the American League.

double play: two outs in one play, for example, a strikeout and a base runner being thrown out, or when two runners are called out on the bases.

doubleheader: when two teams play twice on the same day, one game after the other.

earned run average: ERA is a pitching statistic that measures the average number of earned runs scored against a pitcher for every nine innings pitched.

error: a defensive mistake resulting in a batter reaching base or getting extra bases. The official scorer calls errors.

fastball: a pitch thrown at high speed, usually more than 90 miles per hour (145 km/h) in MLB.

foul ball: when the ball is hit into foul territory. A hitter's first two fouls count as strikes, but a batter can't be called out on a foul ball.

Gold Glove Award: the Gold Glove is given annually to the player at each position in both the American and National Leagues deemed to have exhibited superior fielding performance in the regular season. Votes cast by the team managers and coaches determine the award winner.

grand slam: a home run when runners are on all the bases.

ground-rule double: when a ball is hit fairly but then goes out of play (e.g., over the home run fence after it bounces) but because of an agreed-upon rule for the ball park, the player gets to second base.

hit-and-run: a play in which a base runner runs right when the pitcher pitches, and the hitter tries to hit the ball into play to help the runner get two bases or avoid a double play.

knuckleball: a pitch with as little spin as possible that moves slowly and unpredictably. The pitcher grips the ball with his fingertips or knuckles when throwing the pitch.

line drive: when a batter hits the ball hard and low into the field of play, sometimes called "a rope."

Most Valuable Player Award: the MVP award is given annually to the player in each of the American and National Leagues deemed to be the most valuable to his team in the regular season. The award winner is determined by votes cast by the Baseball Writers' Association of America, a professional association for baseball journalists.

no-hitter: a game in which one team gets no base hits.

pickoff: when a pitcher or catcher throws a runner out, catching him or her standing off the base.

relief pitcher: a pitcher who comes into the game to replace another pitcher.

sacrifice: when a batter makes an out on purpose to advance a runner (e.g., a sacrifice bunt or fly ball). A sacrifice play is not an official at bat for the hitter.

Silver Slugger Award: given annually to the player at each position in each of the American and National Leagues deemed to be the best offensive player in the regular season. Votes cast by the team managers and coaches determine the award winner.

slider: a pitch that is almost as fast as a fastball but curves. The pitcher tries to confuse the batter, who may have trouble deciding what kind of pitch is coming.

stolen base: when a base runner runs right when the pitcher pitches, and if the pitch is not hit, makes it to the next base before being thrown out.

strike zone: the area above home plate where strikes are called. The pitch must be over home plate, above the batter's knees, and below the batter's belt.

strikeout: when a batter gets a third strike, either by missing the ball or not swinging on a pitch that is in the strike zone.

trade deadline: the trade deadline, which typically falls at 4 p.m. ET on July 31, is the last point during the regular season at which players can be traded from one club to another.

walk: when the pitcher throws four pitches outside the strike zone (called balls by the umpire) before throwing three strikes, allowing the hitter to walk to first base.

WAR: this acronym stands for Wins Above Replacement. It is an advanced statistics metric designed to measure the value of a player by indicating how many games a player adds to a team's win total versus those that would be added by the best available replacement player. For position players, the formula is WAR = (Batting Runs + Base Running Runs + Fielding Runs + Positional Adjustment + League Adjustment + Replacement Runs) / (Runs per Win). For pitchers, the formula is WAR = [[([(League "FIP" − "FIP") / Pitcher Specific Runs per Win] + Replacement Level) (IP/9)] Leverage Multiplier for Relievers] + League Correction.

wild pitch: A pitcher is charged with a wild pitch when his pitch is so errant that the catcher is unable to control it and, as a result, the base runner(s) advance.

FURTHER READING

Cohen, Robert. *The 50 Greatest Players in Detroit Tigers History.* Lanham, MD: Taylor Trade Publishing, 2015.

Holley, Joe. *Hurricane Season: The Unforgettable Story of the 2017 Houston Astros and the Resilience of a City.* New York: Hachette Books, 2018.

Houston Chronicle. *Astros Strong: Houston's Historic 2017 Championship Season.* Chicago, IL: Triumph Books, 2017.

Reiter, Ben. *The New Way to Win It All.* New York: Three Rivers Press, 2019.

Smith, Brian. *Liftoff! The Tank, the Storm, and the Astros' Improbable Assent to Baseball Immortality.* Chicago, IL: Triumph Books, 2018.

INTERNET RESOURCES

https://www.mlb.com/
The official website of Major League Baseball.

https://www.mlb.com/astros
The official MLB website for the Houston Astros, featuring team roster, player profiles, statistics, and news.

https://www.cbssports.com/mlb/teams/HOU/houston-astros/
The web page for the Houston Astros provided by CBSSports.com, providing the latest team and league news, schedule, stats, roster, transactions, and more.

https://www.espn.com/mlb/team/_/name/hou/houston-astros
ESPN's web page for the Houston Astros that has team and league content.

https://sports.yahoo.com/mlb/
The official website of Yahoo! Sports' MLB coverage, which includes news, stats, and information on all teams.

https://bleacherreport.com/mlb
The official website for Bleacher Report's coverage of all MLB teams.

https://www.baseball-reference.com/
Baseball resource provided by Sports Reference LLC featuring statistics on past and present players.

https://www.chron.com/sports/
The web page of the *Houston Chronicle's* coverage of the Houston Astros.

INDEX

INDEX

INDEX

AUTHOR BIOGRAPHY

Greg Bach is an avid sports fan, author, and father. He enjoys watching and participating in many types of sports, including football, basketball, baseball, and golf. He enjoyed a brief career as a punter and defensive back at NCAA Division III Carroll College (now University) in Waukesha, Wisconsin, and spends much of his time now watching and writing about the sports he loves.

PHOTO CREDITS

PHOTO CREDITS

EDUCATIONAL VIDEO LINKS

Chapter 1:

http://x-qr.net/1KwP

http://x-qr.net/1LDx

http://x-qr.net/1LiE

http://x-qr.net/1JV8

http://x-qr.net/1Js6

http://x-qr.net/1LG1

http://x-qr.net/1K0m

http://x-qr.net/1Lzs

Chapter 2:

http://x-qr.net/1MAz

Chapter 3:

http://x-qr.net/1J75

Chapter 4:

http://x-qr.net/1KC1

Chapter 5:

http://x-qr.net/1M8b